BATS

FISHERMAN BATS

Pamela J. Gerholdt

ABDO & Daughters

Published by Abdo & Daughters, 4940 Viking Drive, Suite 622, Edina, Minnesota 55435.

Library bound edition distributed by Rockbottom Books, Pentagon Tower, P.O. Box 36036, Minneapolis, Minnesota 55435.

Printed in the United States.

Cover Photo credit: Animals, Animals
Interior Photo credits: Animals, Animals pages 5, 7, 11, 13, 15, 19
Merlin D. Tuttle Bat Conservation International pages 9, 17, 21

Edited by Julie Berg

Library of Congress Cataloging-in-Publication Data

Gerholdt, Pamela J.
    Flsherman bat / Pamela J. Gerholdt.
        p.   cm. — (Bats)
Includes bibliographical references (p.23) and index.
    ISBN 1-56239-501-7
1. Noctilio—Juvenile literature. [1. Fisherman bats. 2. Bats.] I. Title.
II . Series: Gerholdt, Pamela J. Bats.
QL737.C56G47 1995
599.4--dc20   95-7055
                                                          CIP
                                                          AC

About The Author

Pam Gerholdt has had a lifelong interest in animals. She is a member of the Minnesota Herpetological Society and is active in conservation issues. She lives in Webster, Minnesota with her husband, sons, and assorted other animals.

Contents

FISHERMAN BATS

There are over 900 **species** of bats in the world. Fisherman bats are called "New World" bats because they are found in Central and South America. They have short, **water-repellent** fur on their heads and bodies.

Fisherman bats are pale to dark orange, or brown to grayish brown on top, with a lighter line down the middle of their backs, and whitish or bright orange bellies. As the name suggests, fisherman bats catch fish.

All bats are **mammals**, like dogs, cats, horses, and humans. But bats do something no other mammal can do—they can fly!

Fisherman bats have water-repellent fur, allowing them to fly into the water to catch their prey.

WHERE THEY'RE FOUND

Bats live on all of the world's **continents** except Antarctica, the **polar regions**, and a few ocean islands. Fisherman bats live in Central America, South America, and on many islands in the West Indies.

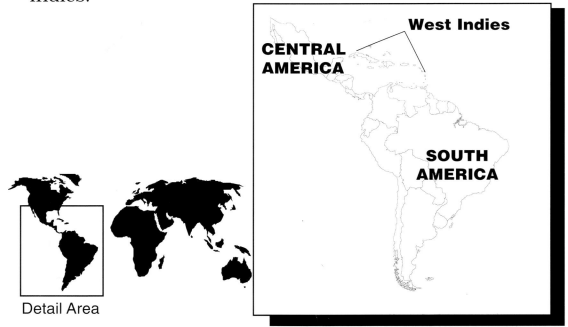

Detail Area

CENTRAL AMERICA

West Indies

SOUTH AMERICA

**A fisherman bat catching a fish in Belize,
Central America.**

WHERE THEY LIVE

Fisherman bats live in **tropical** areas near streams, rivers, lakes and oceans. They **roost** in dark caves, cracks in rocks, and hollow trees in groups of up to 30 bats. The roosts can often be found because of the bats' strong smell.

Bats roost by hanging upside down by their feet. It's easy for them since they have 5 toes with sharp claws, and knees that point backwards!

Fisherman bats roost in caves, cracks in rocks, and in hollow trees.

SIZES

Fisherman bats are 4 to 5.5 inches (98 to 132 mm) long and weigh 2 to 2.75 ounces (60 to 78 grams). They have a **wing span** of about 1.5 feet (.5 meters).

Some bats are much bigger. Large fruit-eating bats such as flying foxes can grow to over 16 inches (40 cm) long with a wing span of over 5.5 feet (165 cm)!

Some bats are very tiny, like the Kitti's hog-nosed bats, that only grow to 1 inch (2.5 cm) long—about the size of a large bumble bee! Although their bodies are small, their wing span is 6.5 inches (16.25 cm).

Fisherman bats have a wing span of about 1.5 feet.

SHAPES

Bats come in many shapes. Fisherman bats have pointed **snouts** with large lips, and **elastic** cheeks that stretch easily. Their ears are large, slender, and pointed. Fisherman bats have wings that are narrow and long—good for flying fast in open areas where they find food. They have well-developed tails, longer than most bats.

Most bats have short tails. A few, like the rat-tailed bats, have long tails. Mountain fruit bats don't have any tails!

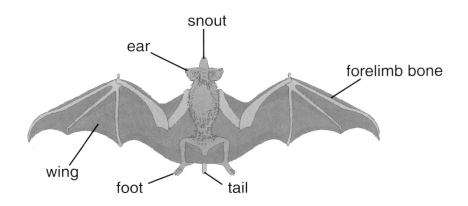

Fisherman bats have large, slender ears and snouts with large, elastic lips.

Bats' wings are made of their extra long fingers and **forelimb** bones that support thin **elastic membranes**. Two membranes, top and bottom, are sandwiched together over the bones on each wing.

SENSES

Fisherman bats have the same five senses as humans. Like over half of all bat **species** they also use **echolocation** to "see" in the dark and find food.

Most bats that use echolocation send out squeaks or clicks through their mouths. Some, like the leaf-nosed bats, send sound out through their nostrils.

HOW ECHOLOCATION WORKS

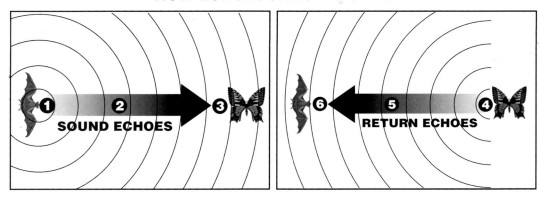

The bat sends out sound echoes (1). These echoes travel in all directions through the air (2). The sound echoes reach an object in the bat's path (3), then bounce off it (4). The return echoes travel through the air (5) and reach the bat (6). These echoes let the bat know where the object is, how large it is, and how fast it is moving.

Fisherman bats use echolocation to "see" in the dark.

DEFENSE

Because they are small, fisherman bats are "bite-sized" for many different **predators.** Cats, dogs, raccoons, and skunks eat bats. So do owls, hawks, falcons, snakes and large frogs. Large spiders eat bats that get caught in their webs. Even worse, some bats eat other bats!

The bat's best defense is to fly away. The fisherman bat's best defense is its narrow, long wings that let it fly away very fast.

Most bats are **nocturnal**, which means they fly at night, avoiding many predators that hunt by day. Bats also find safe, dark places to hide during the day when they **roost**. Most bats have dark colors that make it hard for predators to see them.

The fisherman bat's best defense is to fly away. Its long, narrow wings allow it to fly very fast.

FOOD

Fisherman bats are one of only three kinds of bats known to eat fish. They also eat winged ants, crickets, beetles, and stink bugs. They use their long hind legs and large feet with sharp, curved claws to snatch their food out of the water or air.

Fisherman bats eat their food in flight, or carry it to a **roost** to be eaten while the bat rests. They usually hunt at dusk and during the night. But they have been seen in the late afternoon flying with fishing pelicans. The bats catch the fish the pelicans disturb.

The fisherman bat uses its large feet and sharp claws to hunt for fish.

BABIES

Fisherman bats usually **breed** once a year and have one baby. Or they may breed twice a year, having one baby each time.

The baby bats are very big when they are born. They often weigh 25 percent of their mother's weight. Mother bats take good care of their babies.

Because bats fly, most people think bats are birds that lay eggs. But since bats are **mammals**, their babies are born live.

The fisherman bat in flight.

GLOSSARY

BREED - To produce young; also a type or kind.

CONTINENT - One of the 7 main land masses: Europe, Asia, Africa, North America, South America, Australia and Antarctica.

ECHOLOCATION (ek-o-lo-KA-shun) - The use of sound waves to locate objects.

ELASTIC (e-LAS-tik) - Able to return to its normal shape after being stretched or bent.

FORELIMB - A front limb of an animal.

MAMMALS (MAM-elz) - Animals with backbones that nurse their young with milk.

MEMBRANES (MEM-branz) - Thin, easily bent layers of animal tissue.

NOCTURNAL (nok-TUR-nul) - Active by night.

POLAR REGION- Either the Arctic (north pole) or Antarctic (south pole) regions.

PREDATOR (PRED-uh-tor) - An animal that eats other animals.

ROOST - A place, such as a cave or tree, where bats rest during the day; also, to perch.

SNOUT - The nose and jaws of an animal.

SPECIES (SPEE-seas) - A kind or type of animal.

TROPICAL (TROP-i-kull) - Very hot and humid.

WATER-REPELLENT - Something that keeps water off or out.

WING SPAN - The distance from the tip of one outstretched wing to the other.

BIBLIOGRAPHY

Fenton, M. Brock. *Bats.* Facts On File, Inc., 1992.

Findley, James S. *Bats, A Community Perspective.* Cambridge University Press, 1993.

Johnson, Sylvia A. *The World Of Bats.* Lerner Publications Company, 1985.

Nowak, Ronald M. *Walker's Bats Of The World.* The Johns Hopkins University Press, 1994.

Index